LIVING WELL

SAFETY AROUND
STRANGERS

by Lucia Raatma

THE CHILD'S WORLD®
CHANHASSEN, MINNESOTA

Published in the United States of America by The Child's World®
PO Box 326, Chanhassen, MN 55317-0326
800-599-READ
www.childsworld.com

Subject Consultant:
Bridget Clementi,
Safe Kids Coordinator,
Children's Health
Education Center,
Milwaukee, Wisconsin

Photo Credits: Cover/frontispiece: Corbis; cover corner: Image Source/Punchstock.
Interior: Corbis: 7 (Jose Luis Pelaez Inc.), 9 (Walter Hodges), 13 (Chuck Savage), 19 (Bob Krist), 20 (AFP), 26 (LWA-Dann Tardiff), 27 (Ted Horowitz); Getty Images: 5 (Brand X Pictures/Andersen-Ross), 6 (Photographer's Choice/Dave Nagel), 12 (Taxi/David Sacks), 29 (The Image Bank/Dan Bigelow); Getty Images/The Image Bank/Yellow Dog Productions: 10, 15; Getty Images/Stone: 8 (Sean Murphy), 14 (David Oliver), 16 (Steven Peters), 18 (David Roth), 21 (Robert E. Daemmrich); PhotoEdit: 11 (Tony Freeman), 23 (Mark Richards), 24 (Jeff Greenberg), 25 (Robert Brenner); PictureQuest: 4 (John Wald/Stock, Boston Inc.), 17 (Stockbyte), 22 (Murray & Associates, Inc./Picturesque).

The Child's World®: Mary Berendes, Publishing Director

Editorial Directions, Inc.: E. Russell Primm, Editorial Director; Katie Marsico, Line Editor; Matt Messbarger, Editorial Assistant; Susan Hindman, Copy Editor; Sarah E. De Capua, Proofreader; Katherine Trickle and Stephen Carl Wender, Fact Checkers; Tim Griffin/IndexServ, Indexer; Cian Loughlin O'Day, Photo Researcher; Linda S. Koutris, Photo Selector

The Design Lab: Kathleen Petelinsek, Design; Kari Thornborough, Page Production

Library of Congress Cataloging-in-Publication Data
Raatma, Lucia.
   Safety around strangers / by Lucia Raatma.
     v. cm. — (Living well)
   Includes bibliographical references and index.
   Contents: A day at the park—Who is a stranger?—The people in your neighborhood—On the phone or internet—Strangers at your school—Keeping yourself safe—Glossary—Questions and answers about strangers and safety—Helping a friend learn about strangers and safety—Did you know?—How to learn more about strangers and safety.
   ISBN 1-59296-244-0 (library bound : alk. paper)
   1. Safety education—Juvenile literature. 2. Children and strangers—Juvenile literature. 3. Abduction—Prevention—Juvenile literature. [1. Safety. 2. Strangers. 3. Kidnapping—Prevention.]
I. Title. II. Living well (Child's World (Firm))
  HQ770.7.R27 2005
  613.6'083--dc22   2003027216

TABLE OF CONTENTS

CHAPTER ONE

A Day at the Park

It was a warm, sunny day, and Joseph was enjoying the neighborhood park. His mom was on a bench across the pond. She was holding Joseph's little brother and talking to a friend. Joseph went

It's fun to spend a day at the park with your mom or dad. If you follow a few simple rules, you can stay safe and have a good time.

Joseph was swinging when a man approached him about a lost puppy. Although he wanted to help, he realized he needed to be careful when talking to a stranger.

back and forth on his swing, pumping his legs harder each time.

Then he heard a voice behind him say, "Young man, I have lost my little black puppy. Could you help me find him?"

Joseph turned to see a man standing near the swings. He was holding a leash and looked upset. Joseph loved puppies, and he hated to think that one was lost. But this man was a stranger. His mom had always told him to be careful around strangers. He remembered her saying that sometimes they try to trick you.

Joseph looked at the man. Then he looked at his mom on the bench. She was still talking to her friend.

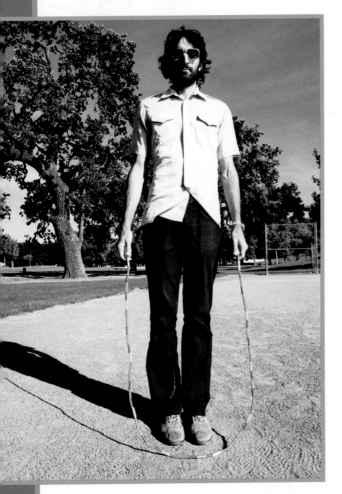

Some strangers are nice, but it is still a good idea to be cautious around people you do not know.

"I'm sorry about your puppy," Joseph said. He got off the swing and started moving away from the man. "But I am not allowed to go anywhere with strangers." Then he pointed to the bench. "My mom has a cell phone if you want to call a friend to help you. Or maybe the police can help."

If a stranger makes you feel uncomfortable or pressures you in any way, yell for help.

Suddenly, the man looked nervous. "Uh, no, that's OK," he

answered. Now Joseph was sure the man had tried to trick him.

"Mom!" he yelled, as he jumped off the swing and ran toward

her. "That man wanted me to go with him!"

Joseph's mother looked up and saw the man run into the trees.

She used her cell phone and called 9-1-1. Police officers arrived

When you call the police about a stranger, try to give them a detailed description of that person.

within a few minutes. Joseph and his mom gave a description of the

man to the police.

"Good job," one police officer told Joseph. "You did the right

thing and stayed safe."

CHAPTER TWO

WHO IS A STRANGER?

You see strangers every day. Your postal carrier is probably a

stranger. So are many of the people you see in the grocery story

or the park. Strangers are people you either do not know or do

Even if you see someone every day, that person may be a stranger. Although the postal carrier regularly brings mail to your house, you probably do not know him very well.

not know well. Your next-door neighbors are probably not

strangers. And your best friend's parents are probably not

strangers. But the people who just moved in across the street are

strangers until you and your

family get to know them.

Your parents can help

explain who strangers are.

Most strangers are nice.

They might say hi to you. If

you are with your parents or

another adult, it is OK to

say hi back. But if you are

by yourself or with other

Walking to school with a group of your friends is a good idea, but you still should avoid talking to strangers.

kids, never talk to strangers.

Making a Safe List

Sit down with your parents and talk about all the people you know who are not strangers. Then make a list of all these people. The list would include everyone in your family. It might include some neighbors, teachers, and other friends. Ask your parents to explain who strangers are—even those whose names and faces you might know.

Then talk about safe places you can go if you are in trouble. Make a list of these places. They might include the police station, fire department, or even the coffee shop on the corner. You will feel safer if you have a list of people you trust and good places you can go if you are scared.

CHAPTER THREE

THE PEOPLE IN YOUR NEIGHBORHOOD

You probably know the faces of most of the people in your neigh-

borhood. You and your family may be good friends with

a lot of your neighbors.

It is a good idea to be

familiar with who lives

in your neighborhood. If

you are, you will be

more likely to notice a

stranger who perhaps

does not belong there.

It is a sad truth that

Try and get to know the people who live near you—it will make your neighborhood a friendlier and safer place.

some people try to

It's scary that some people try to break into other people's houses. Although this is frightening, you can stay safe by talking to your parents about whom you can trust.

hurt others. Someone may try to break into your home. Or

someone may try to kidnap you or other children. That's why

it is important to know whom you can trust. Talk to your

parents about the people in your neighborhood. They can help

you understand which people are strangers and which people

are friends.

Be extra careful if you're home alone and a stranger comes to the door. Unless you're expecting a visitor, it might be a good idea not to open the door at all.

If a stranger comes to your door, follow some rules before deciding to open the door. If either your parents or a babysitter is there with you, ask what to do. But if you are home alone, you must be extra careful. If you are not expecting a visit from a family member or a friend, consider not going to the door at all. If you are expecting such a visitor, you must be careful. Without opening the door, ask who is there.

If it is your best friend or a family member, it is OK to open the door. If the person claims to be a police officer, ask to see a **badge.** The police officer can show it through a window. If the person has a delivery, instruct her to leave it by the door. If

If you're home alone and a delivery person comes to the door with a package, have him leave it outside.

she needs you to sign for it, tell her to come back later. If the person says she has an **emergency** and needs to use your phone, offer to call 9-1-1 for her. But never open the door for her. If the stranger won't leave, call 9-1-1 right away.

CHAPTER FOUR

ON THE PHONE
OR INTERNET

Strangers don't always appear in person. Sometimes they might

try to contact you on the telephone or through the Internet. If you

are home by yourself, ask your parents ahead of time if you should

answer the phone or just let the answering machine pick up. If you

answer the phone, never tell a stranger that you are home alone.

Your parents might say it's OK to answer the phone when they're not home.
Just remember never to tell a stranger that you're by yourself.

*If you talk to a stranger on the phone, be polite but
never give out too much personal information.*

Instead, just say that your parents are busy. If the person on the

other end of the phone asks for your name, do not give it out.

Instead, you should ask, "Who's calling, please?" If the person refuses

to answer, it is a good idea to hang up. If they do give their name,

offer to take a message but be sure not to give out any personal

While surfing the Internet, you can learn new things and meet new people, but it is important to be careful.

information about yourself. If you ever get a phone call that makes you scared or uncomfortable, tell your parents right away.

Surfing the Internet can be fun. But you need to be careful of the strangers you meet there. Never give out your full name, your address, or the name of your school to anyone you chat with on the Internet. Your Internet pal may say she is a 10-year-old girl. But this person may really be an older man or woman who is trying to trick young boys and girls. And never agree to meet an Internet pal in person, unless you have

your parents' permission. Your parents may agree to the idea, and

they may want to come along. But otherwise, meeting a stranger—

even in a public place—is a **dangerous** thing to do.

Even if you plan on meeting an Internet pal in a public place such as a park,
tell your parents so they can help you be as safe as possible.

CHAPTER FIVE

STRANGERS AT YOUR SCHOOL

Most of the people at your school are not strangers. You probably know the teachers and other students well. But you may not know some of the parents well. And you may not know some of the other workers at school, such as the maintenance workers. Be sure to talk to your parents or teachers about whom you can trust at school.

If a stranger ever comes to your school and says your parents asked him to pick you up, be especially careful. He may be trying to trick you. Talk to your parents

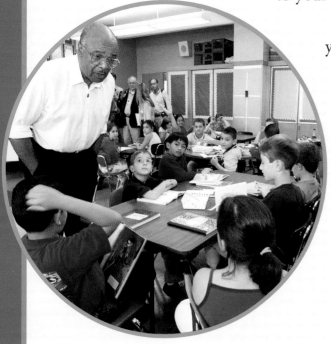

Your teacher and classmates aren't strangers, but some of the other people who work at your school may be.

about a family code word (see the sidebar on pages 26–27). If the stranger does not know the code word, run away from him and tell a teacher immediately.

Also be aware of any strangers hanging around the playground or anywhere near the school. A stranger may try to **lure** you with money, candy, or other food, but do not be fooled by him. And never get into a stranger's car.

If a stranger tells you to get into her car, run away and tell a trusted adult as soon as possible.

KEEPING YOURSELF SAFE

When you are walking in your neighborhood, be aware of every-

thing around you. Avoid shortcuts and stay on streets where you

know people or are familiar with businesses you could go to in case

of an emergency. Notice the people you know

and those you don't know.

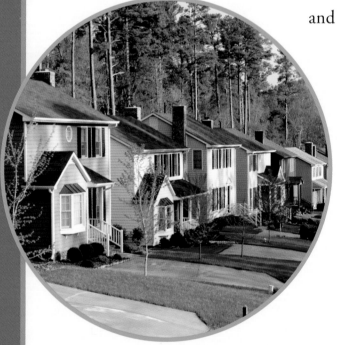

When walking through your neighborhood, try to stay near homes you could run to for help in case of an emergency.

If a stranger approaches you and

you are worried, yell as loudly

as you can. If a stranger

tries to grab you, yell,

"This is not my mom!"

or "This is not my dad!"

That will let other people

Yell as loudly as you can if a stranger tries to grab you or makes your feel uncomfortable.

know you are in trouble. Then run into the nearest public building or to the home of someone you know and trust. A family friend, a clerk in a store, or a waiter in a restaurant can help you call 9-1-1.

If you get lost at a public place such as an amusement park, don't panic.
Calmly go to the information booth or the lost-and-found office.

If you ever get lost or separated from your parents, don't

worry. And don't walk around saying you are lost. Instead, calmly

go to a place that is safe. This could be the information **booth**

at the mall or the lost-and-found office at an amusement park.

The people working at these places will help you find your parents

or the other people you are with.

You may get scared when you think about strangers and how they could trick you. But instead of being afraid, be smart. Take **responsibility** for your own safety. Talk to your parents about any strangers who make you uncomfortable. And ask them about anyone you are unsure of. The more you know about the people around you, the safer you will be.

You should discuss strangers with your parents. They can give you ideas about how to stay safe around them.

Having a Family Code Word

Have you ever had a secret password for a game you were playing? Having a family code word is kind of similar to that. You and your family should pick a word that no one else could easily think of. Only the members of your family will know the word. And your parents will give out the code word only in an emergency and only to people they trust.

Then, if a stranger says your parents asked her to pick you up, you can ask for the code word. Maybe your parents have

to work late or someone in the
family is sick. Or maybe there
has been an **accident.** If the

know you can trust her. If she
doesn't know the word, run
away from her and tell another

Glossary

accident (AK-si-dunt) An accident is an event that takes place unexpectedly and often involves people being hurt.

badge (BAJ) A badge is a small sign with information such as a person's name or title. You usually pin a badge to your clothes.

booth (BOOTH) A booth is a small enclosed area.

dangerous (DAYN-jur-uhss) Something that is dangerous is likely to cause harm. It is not safe.

emergency (i-MUR-juhn-see) An emergency is a sudden and dangerous situation that requires immediate attention.

lure (LOOR) To lure someone is to lead them into danger.

responsibility (ri-spon-suh-BIL-uh-tee) A responsibility is a duty or a job.

Questions and Answers about Strangers and Safety

I've been taught to listen to adults. So if I'm by myself or with friends and an adult in a car asks me for directions, I should help him, right? No! Adults should not ask kids for directions. If the person talking to you is a stranger, it is OK to be impolite. Tell him to ask for directions at a service station. Or ignore him. And stay away from that car!

When I was at the zoo with my dad, a strange woman said she liked my hat. I said thanks. Was that OK? Absolutely. You were with your dad, so you were safe. And the woman was probably just being friendly.

If I call 9-1-1 because someone is hurt and an ambulance arrives, is it OK to let the emergency workers in my home? Of course. You called them for help. Emergency workers are strangers you can trust.

I am home alone and the doorbell rings. The person on the other side of the door says he is here to fix our air conditioner. What should I do? Tell him that he should come back at another time. Your parents would have told you if he was expected, and you should not have the repairman there without another adult present. Don't let him know that you are by yourself. If he won't go away, call 9-1-1.

Helping a Friend Learn
about Strangers and Safety

▸ Role-play with your friend. While one of you acts like a stranger, the other practices how to react. Take turns in each role.

▸ Show your friend your list of people you can trust and safe places you can go (see page 11). Talk to your friend about making the same kind of list.

▸ Tell your friend about your family's code word. Don't tell your friend what the word is, but encourage her to have her family find a good code word, too.

Did You Know?

▸ If you are alone or just with friends, you should always stay at least two arm lengths away from a stranger.

▸ It is a good idea to tell your parents if someone on the Internet asks to meet you in person.

▸ Little kids aren't the only ones who should follow the rules for staying safe around strangers. Big kids and even teenagers should follow the same rules.

▸ You may someday find yourself in an emergency situation where you have no choice but to ask a stranger for help. In this case, local business owners or mothers with young children are people you could possibly trust.

How to Learn More about Strangers and Safety

At the Library

Chaiet, Donna, and Francine Russell. *The Safe Zone: A Kid's Guide to Personal Safety.* New York: Beech Tree, 1998.

Girard, Linda Walvoord. *Who Is a Stranger and What Should I Do?* Morton Grove, Ill.: Albert Whitman, 1985.

Sanders, Pete. *Personal Safety.* Brookfield, Conn.: Millbrook Press, 1998.

Sherman, Josepha. *Internet Safety.* Danbury, Conn.: Franklin Watts, 2003.

On the Web

Visit our home page for lots of links about strangers and safety:
http://www.childsworld.com/links.html

Note to Parents, Teachers, and Librarians: We routinely verify our Web links to make sure they're safe, active sites—so encourage your readers to check them out!

Through the Mail or by Phone

Federal Bureau of Investigation
Crimes against Children Program
935 Pennsylvania Avenue NW
Room 11163
Washington, DC 20535
202/324-3666

KlaasKids Foundation
PO Box 925
Sausalito, CA 94966
415/331-6867

National Crime Prevention Council
1000 Connecticut Avenue NW
13th floor
Washington, DC 20036
202/466-6272

National SAFE KIDS Campaign
1301 Pennsylvania Avenue NW
Suite 100
Washington, DC 20004
202/662-0600

Index

About the Author

Lucia Raatma received her bachelor's degree in English literature from the University of South Carolina and her master's degree in cinema studies from New York University. She has written a wide range of books for young people. When she is not researching or writing, she enjoys going to movies, practicing yoga, and spending time with her family. She lives in New York.